THE
LAKE DISTRICT

CONTENTS

Keswick	2
Derwent Water	6
Castlerigg Stone Circle	12
Borrowdale	14
Buttermere	20
Crummock Water	22
Bassenthwaite	26
Windermere	28
Bowness	30
Ambleside	34
Rydal	36
Elterwater	38
The Langdales	40
Grasmere	44
Ullswater	48
North Lakeland Villages	56
Northern Fells	64
Coniston	68
Hawkshead	72
Lakeside	74
Duddon Valley	80
Wasdale	84
Eskdale	90

MYRIAD
LONDON

Keswick

Backed by Skiddaw and overlooking Derwent Water and the north Lakeland fells, Keswick is the ideal base for exploring the northern Lakes.

I N A SUPERB POSITION, overlooking Derwent Water and the north Lakeland fells, Keswick plays host to a large number of visitors throughout the year. The town is the undisputed hub of the northern Lake District and is an ideal stopping off point for visitors to the northern lakes. Keswick's industrial origins as a mining town are now largely forgotten, but it retains many interesting buildings connected with its history.

From the boat landings (below) it is possible to hire a rowing boat or take one of the many pleasure trips around the lake. There are splendid views of Cat Bells, Skiddaw and the many islands that grace Derwent Water including St Herbert's Island and Lord's Island, both of which are owned by the National Trust.

AROUND KESWICK The Moot Hall (above) in Market Square dates from 1813, and is Keswick's best known landmark. It houses the tourist information centre and, at its west end, there is the famous "one-handed clock".

In the past the hall served as a courthouse, a museum, a prison and a local market. The bell in the tower bears the date 1601 and the letters HDRO. It is thought that this came from the ancestral home of the Derwentwater family on Lord's Isle, one of four islands on Derwent Water.

The Keswick Launch Company runs cruises around Derwent Water starting at the Keswick boat landing and calling at six other landing stages around the lake. The round trip takes around 50 minutes or you can stop off at one of the landing stages to allow access to sights such as Cat Bells, Ashness Bridge and Borrowdale.

Fitz Park (left and above) has a superb setting on the banks of the river Greta. In 2001 the cricket ground in the park, with its wonderful backdrop of Skiddaw, won the Wisden accolade of "the most beautiful ground in Britain".

Sunset over High Crag (below) viewed from the Keswick landing stage.

Derwent Water

Located beneath the fells of Cat Bells and Skiddaw,
Derwent Water boasts stunning scenery and lakeside walks.

DERWENT WATER With the bustling town of Keswick on its northern shores, Derwent Water is one of the larger of the lakes in the region – at its widest point it is just over a mile wide. Seen at dawn, the view from Friar's Crag (previous page) across to Borrowdale was a favourite of the writer John Ruskin. Visitors can enjoy it by taking a short stroll past Keswick's landing stages. The view (above) is from the peak of Cat Bells with the massive bulk of Skiddaw and Blencathra looming behind Keswick. The little hill of Castlehead, close to Keswick, provides a view (left) to the west towards Cat Bells and Causey Pike.

DERWENT WATER DAWN
This view is from Friar's Crag, a short distance from the landing stages at Keswick. The crag juts out into the lake giving an unbroken view across Derwent Water to the Jaws of Borrowdale. Friar's Crag has a memorial to the writer John Ruskin who described the view as one of the three most beautiful scenes in Europe.

ASHNESS BRIDGE Taken on a morning in February, ice has formed on the rocks of Barrow Beck (below) which flows under this ancient packhorse bridge on the road to Watendlath. From here the lake is only visible in the far distance; rising behind it is the Skiddaw massif, partially topped with snow. In the days before motor transport, packhorse bridges such as Ashness were common, particularly in upland areas where streams could easily flood during wet weather. They were designed to accommodate horses in single file loaded with side-bags so there is often very little room for modern vehicles. This treasured view is photographed by thousands of people every year.

Castlerigg Stone Circle

Situated south of Keswick, the mysterious Castlerigg is one of Britain's most important neolithic monuments.

S OUTH OF KESWICK the Castlerigg Stone Circle sits in a natural amphitheatre of hills, with panoramic views of the surrounding fells. It is thought that the circle, which dates from around 3000BC, originally consisted of 70 stones. Today there are 38 stones which form a rough oval, within which there is an unusual small rectangular setting of another 10 stones. Little is known about the origins of Castlerigg although some people have speculated that it may have been an astronomical observatory and a place for meeting and trading. When snow is on the ground (above) the circle takes on an almost other-worldly air and the surrounding mountains, such as Helvellyn, seem to crowd in around the stones.

ST KENTIGERN The parish church of St Kentigern is located at Crosthwaite on the western edge of Keswick. Dating from the 16th century the building is the oldest in the town. Canon Hardwicke Drummond Rawnsley (1851-1920), the co-founder of the National Trust, was vicar here for 34 years, and there is a memorial to him in the baptistry. Canon Rawnsley is also buried here and it is particularly fitting that he lies at rest close to much of the countryside that he helped preserve. The poet Robert Southey, a close associate of Wordsworth and fellow poet, is buried near the north side of the tower. Inside the church there is also a white marble monument to him with an inscription written by Wordsworth.

Borrowdale

Stretching from the head of Derwent Water south to
Seathwaite, Borrowdale is walled in by steep crags on all sides.

T HE TINY VILLAGE of Grange-in-Borrowdale is located near the southern end of the lake. A short distance upstream the "jaws of Borrowdale", where the valley squeezes between Grange Fell and Castle Crag, leave just enough room for the road and river to snake through.

The low-slung twin arches of Grange Bridge (left) span the two branches of the river Derwent that flow either side of a small island, a popular spot for children to play on a summer's day. Most buildings in the area are constructed from green slate and the slate, pebbles and stones that line the riverbed give the clear water a striking blue-green translucence. The Church of the Holy Trinity (below) in the village has an unexpected barrel-shaped ceiling, finished with an unusual saw-tooth design.

ROSTHWAITE This little village is in the Borrowdale valley, on the road from Derwent Water to the Honister Pass. Its working farms, flocks of Herdwick sheep and drystone walls make this a typical Lakeland village. The hamlet is a starting point for many walks, including the one up to Watendlath. The stepping stones (below) across the Derwent can be found on the path from Rosthwaite to Grange. It is little wonder that author and fell-walker Wainwright declared: "A fell walker based in Rosthwaite is like a king with many thrones." The Borrowdale Show takes place in mid September. It is a wonderful opportunity to watch traditional sports, such as fell racing, tug-of-war and Cumberland and Westmorland wrestling.

STONETHWAITE & SEATOLLER This is the only side valley which breaches the great eastern wall of fells in Borrowdale. The two tiny villages of Seatoller and Stonethwaite lie close to each other on the valley floor of Borrowdale. Just to the west the road climbs sharply up the one-in-four gradient of the Honister Pass. The coast-to-coast path links the two villages. Seatoller (top) is little more than a cluster of houses around a farm, but the Yew Tree coffee house makes an ideal stopover for walkers and other visitors. In the graveyard at Borrowdale Church, a simple rough-cast building, is the grave of Bob Graham, the famous fell-runner of the 1930s.

WATENDLATH Situated at the end of an extremely narrow and twisting road from Derwent Water, this little hamlet is best approached on foot, either from Rosthwaite or Ashness – a route which also gives the opportunity of visiting the Lodore Falls on the way. The hamlet consists of a farmhouse or two, one selling teas and another hiring out rowing boats for trout fishing (left). In Watendlath it is possible for tourists to stay on a working farm and witness at first-hand all the seasonal activities of farming life – including sheep-shearing, dipping and gathering.

Buttermere

Situated close to low-lying water meadows, for many people Buttermere is simply the Lake District's most beautiful location.

THIS REMOTE VALLEY can be reached either from the Newlands or Honister Passes. The village is located close to low-lying water meadows where cows were kept, giving Buttermere its name. The view (right) is from the opposite, eastern end of the lake close to Gatesgarth Farm. The popular two-hour walk around the lake is an excellent introduction to the area. The village itself consists of little more than a farm and two hotels, The Bridge and The Fish. The Fish Hotel became famous in the 1790s as the home of Mary Robinson, the innkeeper's daughter, a striking young woman who became known as "The Beauty of Buttermere". Mary features in Wordsworth's poem *The Prelude* and her fame attracted visitors from far and wide.

THE CHURCH OF ST JAMES

The beautifully located Church of St James is perched on a rocky knoll above Buttermere village and has outstanding views of the lake and surrounding high fells. A simple carved stone memorial to Alfred Wainwright, the famous fell-walker and writer, is on one of the church window-sills and there is a view from the window to Haystacks, his favourite mountain and the place where his ashes are scattered. The porch has a functional yet decorative iron gate showing a shepherd with his sheep. The same scene (below) is often played out in real life just outside the church today.

Crummock Water

Situated between the hamlets of Buttermere and Loweswater, Crummock Water has stunning views on all sides.

THE VIEW ABOVE looks across the Loweswater Valley to Crummock Water, sandwiched between the mountains of Grasmoor and Melbreak. In the far distance is the distinctive profile of Great Gable. Loweswater (right) is a small lake which empties into Crummock Water under the gaze of Bunbank and Darling Fell. Rowing boats for fishing belonging to the National Trust can be hired at Watergate Farm, at the southern tip of the lake.

A beautiful path leads to the south-western shore of the lake and after Watergate Farm it passes through the mature native trees of Holme Wood, then continues on to the National Trust bothy.

CRUMMOCK WATER AND RANNERDALE Just across the
fields from Buttermere is the southern end of Crummock
Water. The side valley of Rannerdale (above) leads away
from Crummock Water and is famous for the bluebells
which carpet its slopes in spring. This strategic point was
the site of a battle where Norman invaders were ambushed
and routed by the English. Below, on the right – ablaze with
the glow of dead bracken – is Rannerdale Knotts.
The view (above) shows the forbidding slopes of Melbreak
which dominates the northern end of the lake.

24

Bassenthwaite

One of the largest stretches of water in the Lake District, Bassenthwaite Lake lies at the foot of Skiddaw.

THE VILLAGE OF Bassenthwaite is located down a narrow side road one mile north-east of the lake, well away from the busy tourist centres. Bassenthwaite gives the impression of being an ordinary village without the normal commercial features of a holiday area. This quiet unspoilt charm also extends to the neighbouring villages of Ireby and Uldale. Dash Beck rises "back o' Skiddaw" and cascades over Whitewater Dash; two miles downstream it flows past a grassy area and playground in the village. St John's church lies close to the main road, but another parish church, the ancient church of St Bega, is set in a romantic position surrounded by fields near the lakeshore just north of Mirehouse.

BRAITHWAITE Tucked away at the foot of the Whinlatter Pass two miles west of Keswick, Braithwaite has some of the best walking in the Lakes on its doorstep. The village is a regular starting point for the well-trodden 10-mile Coledale Round. The circular Coledale Round starts from The Royal Oak and includes the summits of Grisedale Pike, Hope Gill Head, Eel Crag, Sail, Sca Crags, Causey Pike, Outerside and Barrow. The walk takes just over six hours and can be tackled by anyone with reasonable fitness.

The spectacular backdrop of Grisedale Pike means that the village enjoys some fine views of the Skiddaw massif. Bassenthwaite Lake is only a stone's throw away. The Coledale Beck adds to the charm of the village, and the many bridges which cross and re-cross the beck make this an ideal spot for walkers. A track leads to the head of Coledale, where mining for barytes and zinc took place until recently at Force Crag Mine. The mine buildings are still clearly visible along with the waste spoil dug from the ground.

Windermere

The largest stretch of water in the Lake District, Windermere is the first stopping-off point for many visitors to Lakeland.

MANY VISITORS catch their first view of the Lake District as they drive over the crest of the hill on the road from Kendal. Windermere is the first stretch of water they encounter and the lively village of the same name makes the perfect base for exploring the area. The 11 mile (18km) length of the lake bustles with the comings and goings of small boats and pleasure craft including the *Osprey* (above). Built in 1902, it is one of the historic wooden pleasure cruisers which ply the lake.

The month of September is perfect for enjoying the drifting beauty of the autumn mist that lies over the lakes. The view (above) looks south over Windermere and was taken at dawn from the lower slopes of Loughrigg Fell. Windermere is the longest of all the lakes in the Lake District, and the largest lake in England.

Ferries have criss-crossed Windermere for more than 500 years. In the early days passengers were even expected to help row the boats. About half a dozen small islands are scattered along the length of the lake, adding to its charm. Opposite Bowness Bay are two of the larger islands which almost cut the lake in two – Belle Isle, with its unusual round tower (built in 1774) is particularly attractive. In 1848 the railway came to Windermere despite the opposition of residents such as the poet William Wordsworth. Today Windermere is the only town in the Lake District which can be reached by rail. The curious clocktower (right) is a memorial to the guidebook writer JB Baddeley.

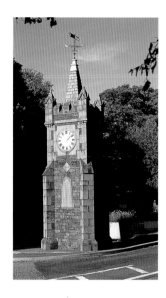

Just off the main road, Queen Adelaide's Hill (below), on the eastern shore of the lake, gives wonderful views of Windermere and the surrounding fells. Queen Adelaide's Hill is one of the national park's seven official viewpoints in the Lakes. The idea for the viewpoints came from Thomas West, who published the first official guidebook to the Lake District in 1778. He described the scenery from a number of viewing points or "stations" which became fashionable places for visitors and artists to gather.

Bowness

Now connected to the town of Windermere, this
quaint lakeside settlement is a tourist hotspot.

O NCE A separate village, Bowness is now connected to the town of Windermere. This bustling setttlement is one of the Lake District's tourist hotspots but it retains a great deal of its original charm. Many of the Victorian mansions built by wealthy industrialists from Lancashire in the 19th century still survive as hotels. The lakefront, with its traditional ticket offices, flowerbeds, ducks and swans still retains much of the flavour of a Victorian resort and is the perfect vantage point from which to enjoy an endless display of boats manoeuvring in and out of the bay.

BLACKWELL HOUSE Just a mile south of Bowness is Blackwell House, one of Britain's most important Arts & Crafts properties. Formerly owned by the Manchester brewer Sir Edward Holt, the house (below) occupies a stunning position overlooking Windermere. It was designed by Baillie Scott who, along with John Ruskin and William Morris, was one of the major exponents of the Arts & Crafts movement.

TROUTBECK The village of Troutbeck stretches for more than a mile along a side road off the Kirkstone Pass that links Windermere and Ullswater. It contains many wonderful examples of Lake District architecture including pubs and stone cottages.

The famous Townend House (owned by the National Trust) is at the southern end of the village. A good example of a wealthy farmer's house, it dates from the 17th century. The village church, unusually just called "Jesus Christ", has a window by Burne-Jones and a churchyard filled with a cheery mass of daffodils in spring.

For many years Troutbeck was the centre of the greatest of annual hound-trailing meetings when thousands of spectators would descend on the village from all over Cumbria.

Ambleside

Surrounded by beautiful mountain scenery, Ambleside lies on the main road that runs between Keswick and Kendal.

AMBLESIDE is a bustling small town with a thriving student community at St Martin's College (now part of the University of Cumbria). The oldest part of the town, the route up to the Kirkstone Pass, has some attractive old houses and streets to explore. Peggy Hill, off North Road and sharply uphill from Stock Bridge, is a good place to start a walk through the town.

Dating from the 17th century, Bridge House on Rydal Road (right) is a National Trust property. Originally a summer house for Ambleside Hall, the building straddles Stock Beck. Beyond it are the old mill buildings complete with waterwheel. Now a restaurant, in the mid 19th century this tiny building was home to the Rigg family – mother, father and six children. In 1926 the house was purchased by local people for a sum of £450 and donated to the National Trust who used it as their first information office.

The centre of Ambleside developed next to Stock Beck, whose fast-flowing waters powered the local watermills. Traces of this history can be seen all around the town. The Water Wheel Shop (below) is a converted mill and still has an intact waterwheel on the outside of the building. The commanding 180ft (55m) spire of St Mary's Church dominates the town. The church was built in 1854 to a design by Sir George Gilbert Scott, the architect made famous by his London buildings including St Pancras station and the Albert Memorial. The famous Lakeland poet William Wordsworth had his office in the town when he was distributor of stamps for Westmorland. He is commemorated, together with his wife and sister, by a memorial chapel and stained-glass window.

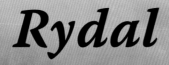

Rydal

The home of William Wordsworth and his family, and separated from Windermere by the tree-lined Rydal Water.

RYDAL IS best-known for its association with the great Romantic poet, William Wordsworth. Rydal Mount (left), one of several characterful houses in the village, was the poet's home for the last four decades of his life. In contrast to the simplicity of Dove Cottage, his previous home in Grasmere, Rydal Mount was grand and spacious. The house is now open to the public and contains beautiful furniture, together with family possessions and portraits. The gardens are laid out as they were when the poet was in residence. Visitors can linger in the Summer House in the grounds, where the poet used to write.

Opposite Rydal Mount is Rydal Hall (right) an imposing 17th century house now owned by the Diocese of Carlisle and used as a conference and retreat centre. The formal gardens are open to the public and there is a little cafe nearby.

RYDAL WATER One of the Lake District's smallest lakes, Rydal Water (left) lies in a sheltered bowl, and early morning mists are common in fine weather. It is one of the smallest lakes and a popular walk leads around its edges hugging the western shore, before crossing the river Rothay on a high-level path that drops into Rydal village past Wordsworth's final home. The Wordsworth family moved to Rydal Mount in 1813 and rented the house for 46 years until the death of Mary Wordsworth in 1859.

Elterwater

This pretty village was formerly a hive of industry with its population working in the local slate quarries. Today it is a popular centre for holidaymakers and a starting point for exploration of Little Langdale.

ELTERWATER lies four miles west of Ambleside and shares its name with the adjacent small lake. This much-visited little village is scenically placed at the entrance to the Langdale valley. The visitor's first view, coming either from Grasmere or Ambleside, is always impressive with the Coniston Fells and Langdale Pikes forming a dramatic background. The village was formerly industrial, and its pretty little slate cottages (above) were built for the workers at the nearby Kirkstone slate quarries. A walking route to Little Langdale takes in views of old and new slate quarries. Later a gunpowder manufacturing business brought workers to the village. The Britannia Inn (below), with its low ceilings and slate floors, is the focal point of the village.

Elterwater is the smallest of the 16 lakes in the Lake District. "Elter" is the Norse word for swan, so Elterwater literally means "Swan Lake". Whooper swans regularly migrate to the lake every winter from Iceland.

The Langdales

The Langdale valleys are famous for their distinctive craggy windswept peaks – known as the Langdale Pikes.

T HE LANGDALES consist of two valleys – Great Langdale and Little Langdale, which join at Elterwater. They are famous for dramatic and varied scenery, and are home to the rocky-topped Langdale Pikes. In the photograph above, the slopes around Little Langdale Tarn are bathed in early morning November sun. This valley retains its traditional character, and only light traffic uses the narrow road to Wrynose Pass. The tarn itself is inaccessible by road but a popular footpath passes over the picturesque little stone Slaters Bridge which crosses the infant river Brathay very soon after it leaves the tarn.

Great Langdale (right) is dominated by the Langdale Pikes which rise abruptly from the level valley floor. The area abounds in colourful names – the Pikes themselves are Pike O' Stickle and Harrison Stickle on the right, while further right is Pavey Arc, Lakeland's biggest cliff, which is cut through by Jack's Rake, a wonderfully challenging trail. Beneath is the sombrely named Dungeon Ghyll and to the left are Crinkle Crags and Bow Fell. Overleaf the view is of Great Langdale in the snow, with the Langdale Pikes in the background.

CHAPEL STILE As the visitor approaches the tiny village of Chapel Stile it seems that with every turn the scenery becomes wilder and more dramatic. The sturdy church, with its fortified tower, serves the whole of Langdale and is a fine sight rising above the village with Silver Howe as a backdrop. The Cumbria Way footpath enjoys the same view as it passes the village. Slate quarrying, both past and present, is evident everywhere from the scree on the fellside, the occasional boom of quarry blasting and the village houses which are almost all built of slate. The local pub, the Wainwright's Inn, is welcoming with open fires and stone-flagged floors.

Grasmere

With its strong literary connections, Grasmere is at the centre
of some of Lakeland's most beautiful landscapes.

AT THE VERY heart of the Lake District, just off the main road from Ambleside to Keswick, lies Grasmere, famous as the home of William Wordsworth for the most creative period of his life. The poet lived at Dove Cottage and its tiny rooms are still much as they would have been when he lived there with his sister, Dorothy, and wife, Mary. The life of the poet, his family and their many visitors is brilliantly described by Dorothy in her diaries.

Looking across the lake from one of the shingle beaches on the southern shore (above) you can see the white face of the Prince of Wales Hotel on the far side. Dove Cottage is just tucked behind to the right. The view shows Helm Crag to the left, the Pass of Dunmail Raise and the soaring slopes of Seat Sandal.

GRASMERE SCENES William, Dorothy and Mary Wordsworth are buried in the Church of St Oswald (above). Their gravestone (right) is a place of pilgrimage for lovers of the Lakeland poets. The rush-bearing festival at Grasmere is celebrated every August on the Saturday nearest to St Oswald's Day. It is a reminder of the time when fresh rushes were strewn each summer to keep unpaved church floors dry and fresh. Dove Cottage (below) lies in the hamlet of Townend on the outskirts of Grasmere.

Grasmere is also home to the famous Grasmere gingerbread. It is sold from the tiny cottage on the edge of St Oswald's churchyard. Built in 1630, the shop was originally the village school. In 1815 Sarah Nelson rented the house and set herself up as a baker and confectioner. Her recipe for gingerbread became famous throughout the area and Grasmere gingerbread is still sold in the shop today.

Ullswater

Famous for its steamers and lakeside walks, Ullswater is regarded by many as the most beautiful of the English lakes.

LOCATED BETWEEN Pooley Bridge in the north and Glenridding in the south, Ullswater stretches for nine miles (14.5km) and makes an elongated "z" shape, giving it three separate reaches of water.

The view (above) of the Pooley Bridge boat-house looks across to Arthur's Pike and Bonscale Pike, both good spots for a quiet fell walk.

Anglers and photographers are generally the only people to be found on the shoreline of the lake, enjoying the dawn (left), where early mist, which gathers across the lake, dissolves gently as the sun rises. This view from Glencoyne looks east towards the slopes of Place Fell, with Hallin Fell beyond.

WORDSWORTH'S DAFFODILS After walking along the Glencoyne shoreline of Ullswater (above), Dorothy Wordsworth wrote in her diary entry of 15th April 1802, "I never saw daffodils so beautiful..." William, her brother, included some of her description in his poem *I wandered lonely as a cloud*. Widely known as "Daffodils", it is probably the most famous poem in the English language. As a result, the Lake District will forever be associated with the flower.

GLENCOYNE FARM The fat chimneystacks (below) are a typical feature of old lakeland farmhouses. There are two theories as to why the stacks were round: one that their shape was better for drawing smoke, the other that, "square ones are better for the devil to hide in". This view is from the path to the former miners' cottages at Seldom Seen, in Glencoynedale. It was a favourite of Queen Victoria, and in the intervening century the view remains little changed.

PATTERDALE On the road between the Kirkstone Pass and Ullswater, the Patterdale valley is a magnet for walkers. Towering above the small village is the Helvellyn mountain range, and one of the most popular routes to the summit lies along the skyline (left). The coast-to-coast long-distance footpath passes through the village, and many walkers use the excellent youth hostel.

The name "Patterdale" harks back to a visit by St Patrick in the 5th century. He landed on the Duddon Sands and travelled to Ullswater, where he preached and baptised the local people. The slate-built church of St Patrick was erected in 1853 by the renowned Victorian architect Anthony Salvin, who also remodelled Muncaster Castle.

GLENRIDDING The largest village on Ullswater, Glenridding lies near the southern end of the lake on the road to the Kirkstone Pass. On weekends, when the weather is good, crowds of walkers leave Glenridding as they set off for Striding Edge. For the less ambitious, the 19th-century Ullswater steamers, *Raven* and *Lady*, will ferry you throughout the year to Howtown or Pooley Bridge.

The southern lakeshore walk from Howtown to Glenridding is reckoned to be one of the best in the Lake District, with constantly changing vistas.

The village owes its existence to the very successful leadmining at Greenside – a mine which closed as recently as the 1950s. The mine made history by being the first to instal electricity, generated by water from Keppel Cove under Helvellyn.

LANTY'S TARN A short, sharp climb from the main car park in Glenridding leads to the lovely, shallow Lanty's Tarn (left). This fairytale stretch of water was named after Lancelot Dobson who owned most of Grisedale. His house, just below the tarn, is now in ruins. Close by is the little knoll of Keldas. From its summit there is a wonderful view across Ullswater almost perfectly framed by Scots pine. A round walk from Glenridding to Fairfield, via St Sunday Crag and returning via Grisedale, passes the tarn which was built to supply water to Patterdale Hall, in the valley below. There is an ice house situated by the small dam wall. The ice was stored in a metal container, and was used during the summer by the residents of Patterdale Hall in their drinks and salads.

POOLEY BRIDGE This bustling village lies close to the northern tip of Ullswater, where the river Eamont leaves the lake, about five miles south of Penrith. Until recently Pooley Bridge was a quiet backwater; now it bustles with visitors and sometimes feels as if it is in danger of being swamped. The narrowness of the old bridge, built for horses and carts, causes major hold-ups as cars try to cross at the height of the summer.

In the 12th century King John granted the village its charter. In the past the village derived its income from farming and fishing, and there is still a thriving business serving the needs of the anglers who fish for the trout, salmon and much rarer schelly (a kind of freshwater herring) that live in these waters. From the village there are walks up onto Moor Divock, an area rich in prehistoric remains which include the ancient Cockpit stone circle. The Ullswater Steamer Company boats link Pooley Bridge with Howtown and Glenridding and connect with walks on the eastern side of the lake.

North Lakeland Villages

Away from the hustle and bustle of Keswick and Derwent Water are a host of pretty unspoilt villages for the visitor to explore.

THE SMALL village of Dacre with its ancient moated castle, pretty cottages, fascinating church and good pub is typical of what the countryside in the northern Lakes has to offer. Dacre lies on a minor road leading from the A66 to Ullswater, six miles south-west of Penrith. Dacre Castle was originally a 14th century pele tower, built to defend the English border against the Scottish reivers. The first floor is known as "the room of the three kings" as it is believed that two Scottish kings and the king of Cumberland met here to sign a peace treaty.

The Norman church of St Andrew's is beautifully cared for by its parishioners. A large stone bear marks each corner of the churchyard. The bears appear to tell the story of a small cat or lynx which jumps onto the bear's back; eventually the bear fights off its tormentor, eats the cat and falls into a contented sleep. Beyond this the origins of the bears and their significance is a puzzle. Inside the church there are many monuments to the Hassell family of Dalemain, the original owners of Dacre Castle, including a superb modern window. Another modern window commemorates Willie Whitelaw, the Conservative politician who is buried at the church. On the floor is an engraved stone, thought to be a Viking grave. The historic house and garden of Dalemain lies just one mile from Dacre. A beautiful mix of medieval, Tudor and Georgian architecture, it was bought by Sir Edward Hassell in 1769.

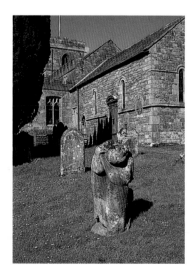

ASKHAM Described by the famous fell-walker Alfred Wainwright as "the most attractive village in Westmorland", Askham lies five miles south of Penrith on the road to Haweswater. Its pretty cottages line an unusually long and wide village green. The road through the village climbs steadily for nearly a mile from Askham church, by the bridge over the river Lowther, to the gateway of Askham Fell. Most of the cottages were built towards the end of the 17th century and many have impressive datestones.

Askham boasts two historic pubs – the 17th-century Queen's Head, with wooden beams, and the 18th century Punch Bowl on the village green. The Punch Bowl was once a watering hole for travellers on their way to the village of Mardale, the village which disappeared after the construction of the reservoir at Haweswater.

At the lower end of the village lies Askham Hall, the family home of Lord Lonsdale. The hall is a mainly Tudor addition to an early defensive pele tower. A short distance from the village is St Peter's Church, built in 1832 and funded by the Earl of Lonsdale, the original owner of Askham Hall. The ruins of Lowther Castle (photograph overleaf) are just across the river – the towers can be seen from the village, rising above woodland. Once the entire village was part of the Lowther Estate. Unusually, one of Askham's main attractions today is a heated outdoor swimming pool.

LOWTHER Situated five miles south of Penrith in beautiful parkland on the eastern fringes of the Lake District lies the spectacular Gothic ruin of Lowther Castle. The estate villages of Lowther New Town and Lowther village lie about half a mile from the castle and church. The castle was built in 1810 for the Lowther family, influential landowners who lived at nearby Askham Hall. The "Yellow Earl", the fifth Lord Lonsdale (1880-1944), was a great character but notoriously extravagant. He hired more than 90 staff for the castle. This high-spending lifestyle eventually broke the family, and by the 1950s the castle fell into disrepair.

HARTSOP This unspoilt village (left) is situated in a sheltered side-valley near Brothers Water at the northern foot of Kirkstone Pass. In the past the area was busy with mining, quarrying and milling and it is worth a short walk along the track to the Hayeswater Reservoir to see the impressive ruins of the watercourse and wheel-pit of the former Mires Head leadmine.

On the return path to the left are the remains of a cornmill together with its grinding stones. The village, like many other Lake District villages, contains a number of narrow alleyways often referred to as "spinning galleries"; these were used for the display and drying of fleeces rather than spinning wool.

ANGLE TARN Not to be confused with the stretch of water of the same name under Bowfell, Angle Tarn (above) lies high above Patterdale and Hartsop. The tarn has a gentler appearance than many other high level lakes since it is attractively cupped by surrounding crags and is unusually indented and reedy. In the far distance are the more northerly stretches of the Helvellyn range.

BROTHERS WATER A short distance outside Hartsop, on the track to Patterdale and Ullswater, is this dramatic view of Brothers Water (below). Hartsop Hall, a picturesque farmhouse dating from the 16th century, can be seen on the far side sheltered by the slopes of High Hartsop Dodd.

Northern Fells

This superb region includes remote Haweswater and the dramatic peaks of Helvellyn and Striding Edge.

Reached by a long narrow road, the Haweswater reservoir was constructed in the 1930s by building the massive dam wall at Burbanks and enlarging the existing lake. The reservoir supplies Manchester with drinking water. The view above shows The Rigg (centre) and Kidsty Pike (right). Submerged beneath the water lies the old village of Mardale, drowned when the valley was flooded.

HIGH STREET A wall runs along the 28 mile length of High Street (right), the course of a Roman road.

STRIDING EDGE The route up to
Helvellyn is one of the most popular walks
in the Lake District. In the summer there
are often hundreds of walkers making
their way to and from the summit.

At the top, Helvellyn is grassy and
remarkably flat, but at the eastern side
of the fell lies the knife-sharp ridge of
Striding Edge (above). The narrow path
along its top has great drops on either side
and can be dangerous. Near the top of the
mountain is the Gough Memorial which
commemorates the death of Charles
Gough, a lakeland tourist who, in 1805,
died whilst trying to cross Striding Edge.
His dog guarded his body for three
months, before he and his master's corpse
were discovered. On the left of the
photograph is Red Tarn, so-called because
it reflects the rosy glow of the dawn.

KIRKSTONE PASS On the road between Windermere and Ullswater lies Kirkstone Pass, the highest mountain road in the Lake District. The name of the pass comes from a large boulder shaped like a church or "kirk", which lies by the side of the road. From the pass there are stunning views towards the high ground of Patterdale and over Brothers Water. In wintry weather the pass is often closed and the resulting snow-drifts take on a deceptively beautifully sculptured appearance when snow is blown into the lee of the walls during blizzards.

Coniston

At the heart of southern Lakeland, this stunning lake and town is rich in literary and sporting connections.

THE OLD MAN OF Coniston dominates the landscape above the town. The slopes of the slate grey mountain are scarred by the legacy of old mineworkings – copper was extracted here for more than 500 years. The farm in the foreground, High Bank Grounds, was the setting for *Swallows and Amazons*. The view on the right is taken on a still September morning with the peaks of the Old Man of Coniston and Weatherlam (right) towering above the village of Coniston. This view from Brantwood, the home of the critic and social reformer John Ruskin, was considered by him to be the finest in the Lake District.

CONISTON The restored steam yacht *Gondola* (below) plies Coniston Water from the pier to Brantwood. The boat combines the workmanship of a Venetian gondola with that of a Victorian steamship.

Brantwood, the home of John Ruskin, is open to the public all year round. It is perched on a narrow shelf at the foot of a steep fell high above Coniston Water. The John Ruskin museum in the town was established as a memorial to Ruskin and is a celebration of the area's heritage. The museum also honours the life of Donald Campbell whose many attempts to break the world water-speed record ended in tragedy on Coniston Water. His gravestone can be seen in Coniston's new cemetery and its shape reflects his famous boat *Bluebird*.

NEAR SAWREY AND ESTHWAITE The villages of Near and Far Sawrey lie one mile apart between Windermere and Esthwaite Water (below). Hill Top, the home of Beatrix Potter, is situated in Near Sawrey making this the better known of the two villages. The house (above), now owned by the National Trust, is open to the public. The author's furniture, china and watercolours are on display.

Hawkshead

Home of the Beatrix Potter Museum, William Wordsworth and his brother were pupils in The Old Grammar School.

S ITUATED MIDWAY between Windermere and the northern end of Coniston Water, this famous village lies just north of Esthwaite Water and near the ever-popular beauty spot of Tarn Hows. It is a compact maze of picturesque whitewashed buildings, dominated by the church of St Michael's and All Angels (above) from its position high on Hawkshead Hill.

Hawkshead is closely linked to the early life of Wordsworth. The poet and his brother John were both pupils at the old grammar school, which was founded in 1585. His desk, covered in carvings done by the two boys, can be seen on view in what is now a museum. As a boy, Wordsworth lodged in the cottage of Anne Tyson (below), half a mile from the village at Colthouse. Anne is said to have had a great influence on him: she was a gifted story-teller and may have sparked an interest in tales of the countryside in the young poet's mind.

The village also houses the Beatrix Potter Gallery, a 17th century building which was once the office of local solicitor William Heelis, who married the author in 1913. Hill Top, the home of Beatrix Potter, bought from the royalties she earned from her first books, is situated close by in Near Sawrey. It is now owned by the National Trust.

LATTERBARROW, BLEA TARN AND THE RIVER BRATHAY A short, sharp climb from Hawkshead leads to the summit of Latterbarrow (below) which gives dramatic panoramic views to the west across Hawkshead to the Coniston Fells. In the near distance is Blelham Tarn with the northern reaches of Windermere in the distance.

Blea Tarn lies on higher ground between the two valleys of Great Langdale and Little Langdale. This bleak winter view shows the Langdale Pikes in the far distance. The waters of the river Brathay flow from Elterwater into Windermere. The Norse word "Brathay" means "broad river".

Lakeside

One mile north of Newby Bridge, this popular spot on Windermere is busy with steam trains and pleasurecraft.

THE STATION PLATFORM and landing stages at Lakeside can be seen above the mass of hawthorn blossom on the slopes of Gummers How (left). Steam trains puff up and down the scenic little railway line which follows the river Leven for 3.5 miles from Haverthwaite. A popular way of extending the trip is to then board one of the boats run by Windermere Lake Cruises. Alternatively, in summer, a little ferry crosses the lake to Fellfoot Park and Garden, owned by the National Trust. This is the perfect spot for a picnic, a visit to the tearoom, or a wander around the Victorian gardens and along the lake shore. The Aquatarium at Lakeside is a popular choice for families – you can be nose to nose with fish and then walk in a tunnel beneath them.

CROSTHWAITE The attractive village church of St Mary's
was built in 1878. The name of the village means "a cross in
a clearing" which may derive from a former chapel on the
same site. The church is situated next to the Punch Bowl,
which dates from the 17th century. In late April the Lyth and
Winster valleys are awash with the white blossom of damson
trees in the little orchards scattered around the area. The
sheltered, warm climate of southern Lakeland is ideal for
growing damsons and each spring the Westmorland damson
association holds a "damson day" at Howe, near Crosthwaite.

CARTMEL The picturesque village of Cartmel lies on a peninsula on the southern edge of the Lake District that reaches into the flat expanse of Morecambe Bay, two miles west of Grange-over-Sands. Cartmel is best known for its ancient priory (above) and also for its racecourse. Horse-racing at Cartmel dates back to 1856 but it is believed that monks from the priory entertained themselves by holding races with mules as early as the mid 15th century. The racecourse hosts the annual agricultural show on the 1st Wednesday in August.

THE PRIORY CHURCH

Cartmel Priory church (left and far left), founded in 1188, towers over the village. The priory was granted to the monks of Lindisfarne by King Egfrith of Northumbria in the 7th century. It was an ideal spot for a monastic retreat, since it was protected to the north by the mountains of the Lake District and to the south by the treacherous sands of Morecambe Bay. Although much of the priory was destroyed by Henry VIII at the time of the Dissolution of the Monasteries, the priory church and the gatehouse in the village square still survive. It is reputed to be the most beautiful church in the north-west of England and every year attracts 60,000 pilgrims and tourists. The interior of the church is vast, but rich in fascinating artefacts, which include a 200 year old umbrella, claimed to be one of the first of its kind in the world. Among the glories of the church are its beautiful stained-glass windows, which include some Pre-Raphaelite panels.

The river Eea winds its way through the village and adds charm to the side streets with their handsome houses. The village square has a fine assortment of 16th to 18th century buildings with characterful pubs and well-stocked shops. The square also boasts the original Market Cross and fish slabs situated close to the water pump where villagers once traded. Cartmel is a magnet for lovers of fine food and on the outskirts of the village there is a farm shop selling food fresh from local suppliers. Cartmel Village Shop (below) on the square is the home of the famous sticky toffee pudding, a delicious but diet-defying treat!

Attractions on offer to the visitor include carriage rides around the village and surrounding countryside.

Duddon Valley

Remote and unspoilt, the beautiful Duddon Valley and its estuary marks the south-western edge of Lakeland.

LOCATED BETWEEN Morecambe Bay and the west Cumbrian coast, the Duddon estuary opens into the Irish Sea just north of Barrow-in-Furness. It has a shoreline of 28 miles. The photograph above is taken from Sandale Haws nature reserve. It is on the edge of the shipbuilding town of Barrow-in-Furness but still offers views of mountains, pale sand and sky that could almost be Hebridean. Black Coombe, lying across the estuary, is detached from the main Lake District mountains, but the views from its summit are hard to beat. The Coniston Fells are seen in the far distance on the right.

HARTER FELL The Duddon Valley, between Coniston and Wast Water, does not contain a lake – perhaps one reason why it remains relatively unvisited. However, the river Duddon, with its rushing water, incredibly clear pools and sparkling waterfalls, is more than ample compensation. The shapely peak of Harter Fell (right) stands at the top end of the valley and is accessible from the roadside at Hardknott Pass. From the summit there are views of both the Scafell range to the north and the Coniston range to the south and east. The tiny villages of Ulpha and Seathwaite are practically the only settlements in the area.

BROUGHTON-IN-FURNESS On the southern tip of the national park, seven miles from Coniston, Broughton is a large village that manages successfully to tread the fine line of catering for its visitors, yet still retains the atmosphere of a local settlement. The handsome square (below) is dominated by chestnut trees which are a beautiful sight in May with their flowering "candles". In the centre of the square is a pair of stocks and an obelisk. On the south side, the 17th century town hall with its seven arches, clock and weather vane, make a superb site for the local tourist information centre.

Broughton Mills (above) with its picturesque pub is a tiny hamlet in an idyllic valley two miles north of Broughton. The small but beautiful Holy Innocents Church is well worth a visit.

Wasdale

Often described as the "wild west", the remote valley of Wasdale and the area around Wast Water is about as far removed from "civilisation" as it is possible to be almost anywhere in England.

CLOSE TO THE west coast of Cumbria, Wasdale is a hidden corner of the Lake District which, due to its remote location, has fewer visitors than other parts of the region. However, there is much for the visitor to enjoy – Wasdale is the home of Scafell Pike, England's highest mountain, its deepest lake, Wast Water and St Olaf's, its smallest church. The photograph (left) is the first view of Wast Water most visitors will see as they approach from the west. On the right can be seen the rounded slopes of Scafell with Scafell Pike behind. Directly ahead are the sheer slopes of Great Gable. The photograph above shows the packhorse bridge which lies behind the Wasdale Head Inn at the far end of the lake.

WAST WATER One of the most distinctive features of Wast Water is the Wasdale Screes which form a dramatic, mile-long wall on the south side of the lake. The overall drop amounts to nearly 2000ft (610m). The entire length of the Screes is riven by steep gullies, which offer challenging routes for the mountaineer.

This dramatic photograph (above) of Wasdale from Great Gable is taken from a vantage point close to the Westmorland Cairn, built in 1876 by two Westmorland brothers to mark what they regarded as the finest mountain viewpoint in the Lake District. It is hard to disagree. Lying a few hundred yards south, and out of sight of the summit of Great Gable, it clings to the mountain's rim above a startling drop.

Quintessentially Lakeland, the central section of this classic view (right) is used as the logo by the Lake District National Park Authority. The grandeur of the surrounding fells is hard to beat, and it is arguably the most dramatic scene in the Lake District. From left to right the fells in view are Yewbarrow, Kirk Fell, Great Gable, Scafell and the Wasdale Screes.

WASDALE HEAD More of a hamlet than a true village, this is the only clutch of buildings for many miles around. Wasdale Head has a magnificent setting just north-east of Wast Water in an arena of dramatic mountains which include Scafell.

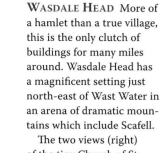

The two views (right) of the tiny Church of St Olaf, close to the track at Wasdale Head, show the same scene at different times of the year. The church is almost entirely surrounded by ancient yews; the path leads to the start of the ascent of Great Gable. In the graveyard there are memorials to climbers, and the interior of the church contains a beautiful stained-glass window showing the dramatic rock formation of

nearby Napes Needle, with the dedication: "I will lift up mine eyes unto the hills, from whence cometh my strength".

The Wasdale Show in early October takes place in fields adjacent to the church. The show features Herdwick sheep and a great variety of traditional sporting events take place, including hound-trailing. The event is one Cumbria's oldest and most popular sports. The dogs follow a trail made of a mixture of paraffin and oil of aniseed. The races take place over a mixture of moorland, fields and fells and, as each race unfolds, many of the owners and spectators bet on the outcome adding to the air of excitement.

NETHER WASDALE (left) is the tiniest of settlements and lies between Gosforth, Santon Bridge and Wast Water. Its attraction lies in its wonderfully skewed ratio of buildings: one church and two pubs nearly out-number all others. The village, sometimes known as Strands, is situated at the foot of a hill with a dramatic view of Wasdale Screes in the distance.

89

This narrow valley linking the heart of the Lake District with the west coast passes England's highest mountain and a dramatic Roman fort.

THE RIVER ESK begins its journey at Great Moss, at the foot of Scafell Pike, and runs past the foot of Hardknott Pass, England's steepest road, down to the sea at Ravenglass. The course of the river takes it from high upland fells down into lush green pastures. The view (above) shows Brotherilkeld Farm and the Upper Eskdale valley from the slopes of Harter Fell. Some of the giants of the Lake District's peaks can be seen at the end of the valley – Scafell, Scafell Pike, Esk Pike, Bowfell and Crinkle Crags.

HARDKNOTT FORT In a dramatic location just above Brotherilkeld Farm, below Hardknott Pass, is the Roman fort of Hardknott (right). Founded under the Emperor Hadrian, the fort guarded the strategic Roman road which ran from the important harbour at Ravenglass on the coast, over the mountains to Ambleside. The fort has commanding views over the mountains and down to the sea.

BOOT Three miles west of Hardknott, Boot is the last settlement up the Eskdale valley. Iron mining in the 19th century enlarged the tiny hamlet. The three-foot gauge railway, known as "La'al Ratty", was built to transport the ore seven miles down to the railway at Ravenglass. The price of iron collapsed and the mining business proved shortlived. The railway looked doomed until it was rescued by a group of enthusiasts who turned it into a major tourist attraction, renamed the Ravenglass and Eskdale Railway.

The parish church of Boot, the 12th century St Catherine's (above) is a little distance from the village across fields, with a lovely setting on the river Esk where stepping stones cross to the further bank. Eskdale Mill, the old village cornmill which dates from the 16th century, stands on the far side of the picturesque packhorse bridge over Whillans Beck. It is one of the few remaining water-driven cornmills in Britain and can usually be seen in operation. Close to the mill pond is a glorious picnic spot.

RAVENGLASS The only coastal village within the Lake District National Park, Ravenglass is situated at a point on the estuary where the rivers Irt, the Mite and the Esk converge.

Ravenglass was originally a Roman supply port and there are significant remains of the old bath-house still standing. Today this characterful little village, with its cheerful front gardens, makes for a worthwhile trip as well as being the terminal for the "La'al Ratty" narrow gauge railway.

The magnificent Drigg Beach (above), just north of the town, was used as a training ground for D-Day mine clearance during the Second World War.

MUNCASTER CASTLE Just south of Ravenglass lies Muncaster Castle, which dominates the Esk Valley for miles around. Described by John Ruskin as "Heaven's Gate" the castle has been home to the Pennington family for 800 years. Dating from the 13th century, the building began life as a pele tower to deter marauding Scots and was gradually extended into a castle. In 1862, the fashionable architect Anthony Salvin was commissioned to rebuild the house and he ingeniously merged the tower and castle into one. Open to the public, the castle is a treasure trove of art and antiques with an owl centre and beautiful grounds.

The 77 acre woodland garden contains a magnificent collection of colourful rhododendrons, camellias and azaleas which are seen at their best in spring and early summer. John Ruskin described the Terrace Walk, which offers spectacular views of the Eskdale valley, as "the gateway to paradise". Recently completed is the Meadow Vole Maze which gives an insight into the world of small mammals.

ENNERDALE WATER The most westerly and remote of the lakes, Ennerdale Water (above) and its surrounding fells seems far distant from the hubbub of tourism which surrounds many of the lakes further to the east. Even in the height of summer there are few visitors. This area's remote location is accentuated by the fact that there are few main roads: access to Ennerdale is by a network of tiny lanes. Even the lake itself is unique in Lakeland by having no paved road following any shoreline.

The lake is dominated by the great cliffs of Pillar Fell, the mountain on the right of the photograph. Pillar Rock is a 500ft (892m) outcrop halfway up the summit. It was here in 1913 that the young George Mallory gained early experience ahead of his attempts to climb Everest during the inter-war years.

ST BEES Four miles south of Whitehaven, St Bees is a popular town. It boasts a remarkable priory, a long sandy beach and a fine sandstone headland. On clear days the Scottish coast and the mountains of the Isle of Man can be seen across the Irish Sea.

The Priory Church of St Bega (above) is renowned for its richly decorated Norman doorway. The priory was established by Bega, an Irish nun, who was shipwrecked here in the 9th century. Close to the church is St Bees School, founded in 1583. The original redstone quadrangle bears the coat of arms of its founder, Edmund Grindal, Archbishop of Canterbury in the reign of Elizabeth I.

The four-mile long St Bees Head (left) is a nature reserve. The coast-to-coast walk starts here and ends at Robin Hood's Bay in Yorkshire, a distance of almost 200 miles.

ST BEES Looking from the headland over the dramatic beach at St Bees, with the village in the foreground and, in the far distance, the mountains on the western fringe of the Lake District. The priory of St Bees, which was founded in 1130, was an important ecclesiastical centre until it was closed by Henry VIII during the Dissolution of the Monasteries in 1539.

First published in 2010 by Myriad Books Limited
35 Bishopsthorpe Road
London SE26 4PA

Photographs and text copyright © 2010 Val Corbett

ISBN   1 84746 352 5
EAN 978 1 84746 352 4

Designed by Jerry Goldie Graphic Design

Printed in China

www.myriadbooks.com